Other Works by Susan Striker Published by Henry Holt

The Anti-Coloring Book® *(with Edward Kimmel)*
The Second Anti-Coloring Book® *(with Edward Kimmel)*
The Third Anti-Coloring Book® *(with Edward Kimmel)*
The Fourth Anti-Coloring Book®
The Fifth Anti-Coloring Book®
The Sixth Anti-Coloring Book®
The Anti-Coloring Book® of Exploring Space on Earth
The Anti-Coloring Book® of Masterpieces
Build a Better Mousetrap

THE MYSTERY ANTI-COLORING BOOK®

Susan Striker

with illustrations by
Sally Schaedler
Susan Striker
Edward Kimmel

An Owl Book
Henry Holt and Company

In loving memory of my mother, who died mysteriously this past year,
but whose love and support stay with me...
and for Bob, who revealed the mystery of second love and new beginnings...
and for Jason, whose first smile solved the mysteries of life for me.

"To know is nothing at all; to imagine is everything."
—Anatole France

ISBN 0-8050-1600-7 (An Owl Book)

Henry Holt books are available at special discounts
for bulk purchases for sales promotions, premiums,
fund-raising, or educational use. Special editions
or book excerpts can also be created to specification.
For details contact:
Special Sales Director, Henry Holt and Company, Inc.,
115 West 18th Street, New York, New York 10011.

First Edition

Printed in the United States of America
Recognizing the importance of preserving the written word,
Henry Holt and Company, Inc., by policy, prints all of its
first editions on acid-free paper. ∞

10 9 8 7 6 5 4 3 2 1

THANKS TO

—Jason Striker for contributing original ideas for activity pages in this book
—Vicki Swarz for helping with research and inspiration
—Chris Tomasino, a loyal agent
—Peter and Leann Popielarski for sharing their childhood mystery books

The Anti-Coloring Book is a registered trademark of Susan Striker.

Introduction

We all love a good mystery! Wondering "whodunnit?" can absolutely make you tingle with anticipation. Looking for the answer can be a lot more fun than knowing what the answer is. Wondering, fantasizing, imagining...therein lies the excitement.

The greatest gifts we can give our children are curiosity and a sense of wonder. We can either help children solve problems by answering the questions for them or we can help them discover the excitement that open-ended questions can contain. We need to challenge young minds and stimulate young imaginations, not just acquaint them with facts and figures. Of course there are many "truths" that growing children need to be taught, but there are many more that they need to discover on their own.

As children look to us for approval, we must give it when they ask questions, not just when they find answers. There is no "right" answer to any of the problems presented in this book. A child can do the same project over and over again and come up with a different "right" answer every time. The curiosity, the drive to solve a problem is the spark we want to kindle. I have tried to present a balance of everyday mysteries with some of the world's bigger mysteries, so you will find everything from cops 'n' robbers to the origin of the universe. You can help expand each experience for your child by letting go of your own preconceived notions. For example, when you get to the page about a Loch Ness monster, forget about any scientific explanations you may have read and set aside the soothing "there is no such thing." Don't provide answers, ask questions! "What does Nessie look like? What does it eat? Does it have a family? Is it big or small, furry or smooth, happy or sad? Do you think it is lonely, or are there more creatures like it in the loch?

I, for one, much prefer wondering about the likelihood of a Loch Ness monster and what it might be like, than knowing for sure that there is no such thing! Wouldn't you?

Paul Romanych, age 10

You have achieved fame and fortune by
solving the mystery of the black hole!

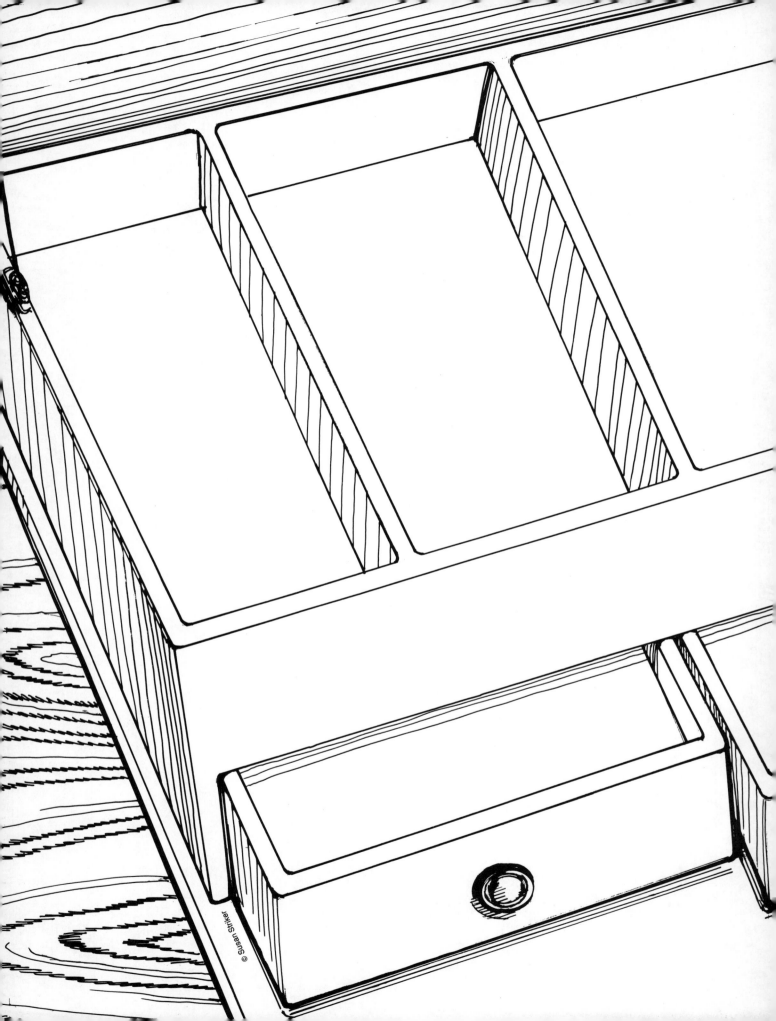

OFFICIAL
BURGLARY REPORT

These imitation jewels were placed in the velvet box to replace the genuine ones, which were stolen.

When the beacon of light swept over the water,
the mystery of the shipwrecks was solved.

© Susan Striker

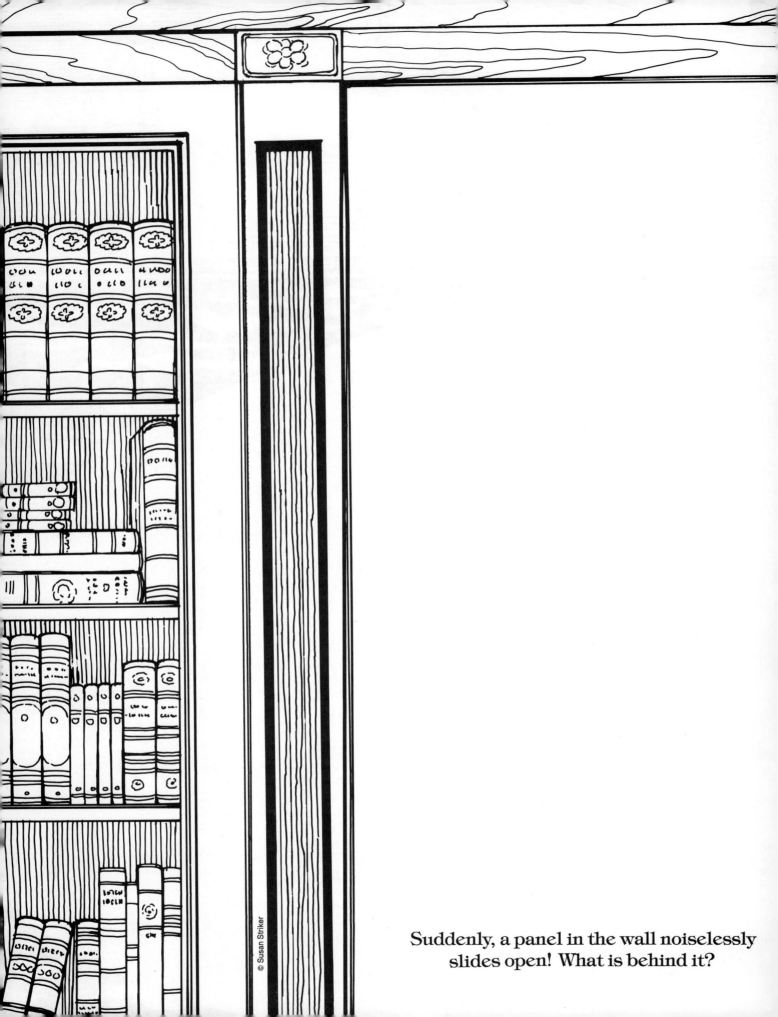

Suddenly, a panel in the wall noiselessly slides open! What is behind it?

© Susan Striker

You have made a startling discovery while skin diving!

MISSING PERSON REPORT

INSTRUCTIONS: Print clearly and legibly

Name _____ Alias _____

Address _____ Telephone number _____

Town or City _____

Male or Female?	Age	Height	Weight	Eyes

Hair _____ Mustache or beard _____ Eyeglasses _____

Moles or scars _____

Draw any tattoos here

Draw any other distinguishing marks here

Clothing _____

Jewelry _____

Draw a Picture of the Missing Person Here

You can help the police by filling out this missing person report.

The flash of lightning revealed a surprise!

© Susan Striker

From your hiding place in the bushes you observe incredible things!

When the Martians landed, you were the only witness in the world. Everyone is clamoring for your drawings and your words to describe the incredible sight you saw.

My Drawing of the Martian

The Martian said...

What made the strange sound that awakened the sleeping child?

© Susan Striker

What is in the mystery package that the butler just delivered?

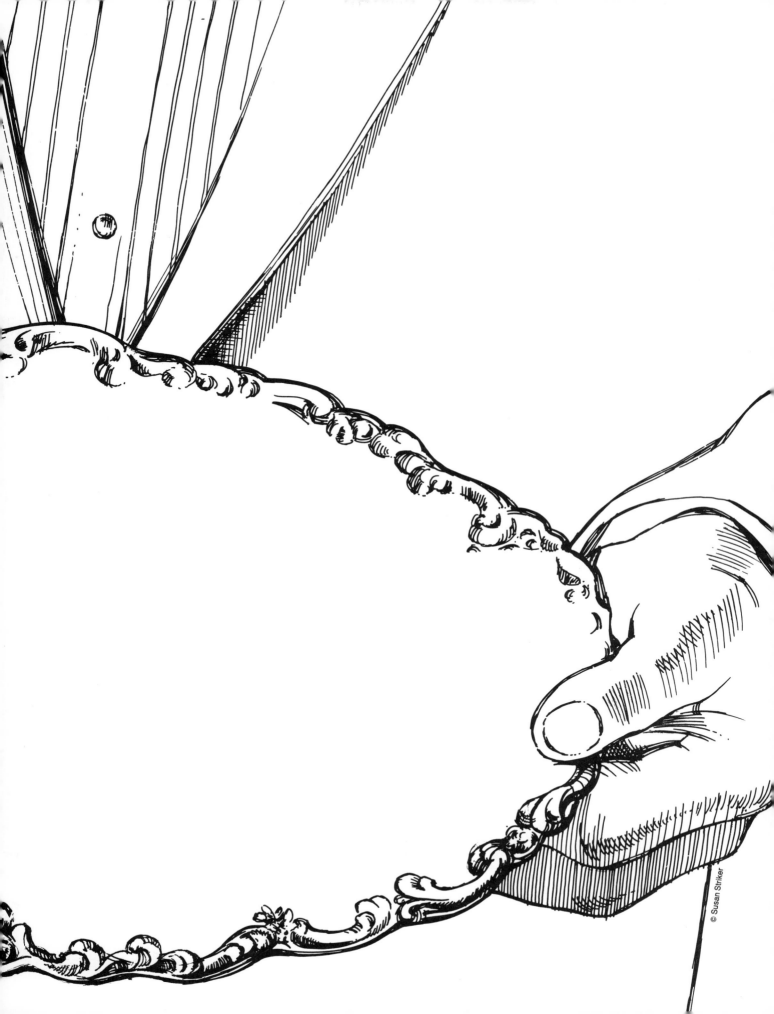

© Susan Striker

gh in the Himalaya Mountains there have been reports of an abominable snowperson.
What does the snowperson look like?

We heard a crackle behind us and stood frozen.

CLUES

Let's see if we can find a clue by looking through the magnifying glass.

© Susan Striker

Suddenly, an apparition appeared at the head of the stair

© Susan Striker

This case was so difficult to solve that the captain
had to call out every available division
of the police force. Who or what are
the police looking for?

What do you spy through
the keyhole of suspense?

© Susan Striker

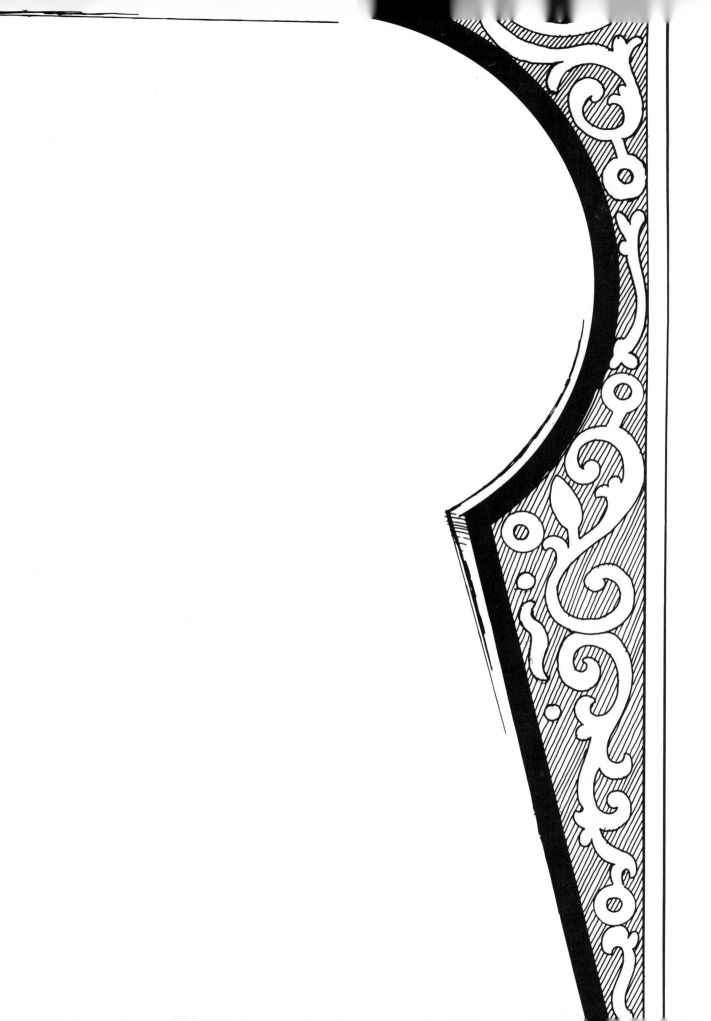

REWARD!

Full Front Portrait

Description of individual _____

_____

_____

_____

_____

If you have seen the whereabouts of the above individual, take no direct action yourself.

$10,000

Profile

Wanted for _____

_____

_____

_____

_____

_____

Simply contact your local FBI office or local police immediately.

You are the only spelunker brave enough

to explore this mysterious cave.

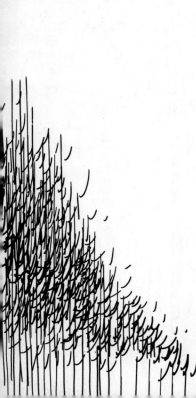

Who or what is behind the billowing curtain?

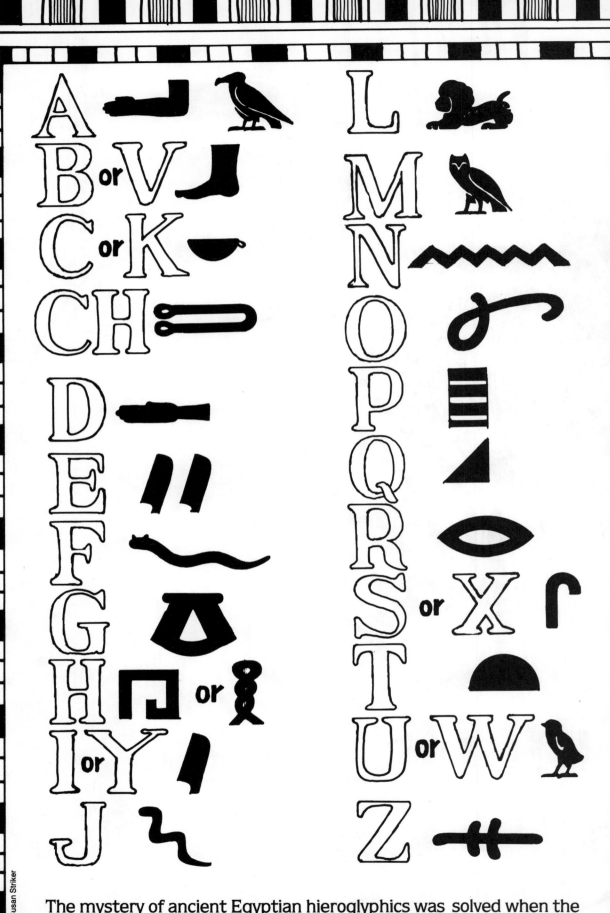

The mystery of ancient Egyptian hieroglyphics was solved when the Rosetta stone was found, providing the key to translation. Can you decode your own name in Egyptian hieroglyphics?

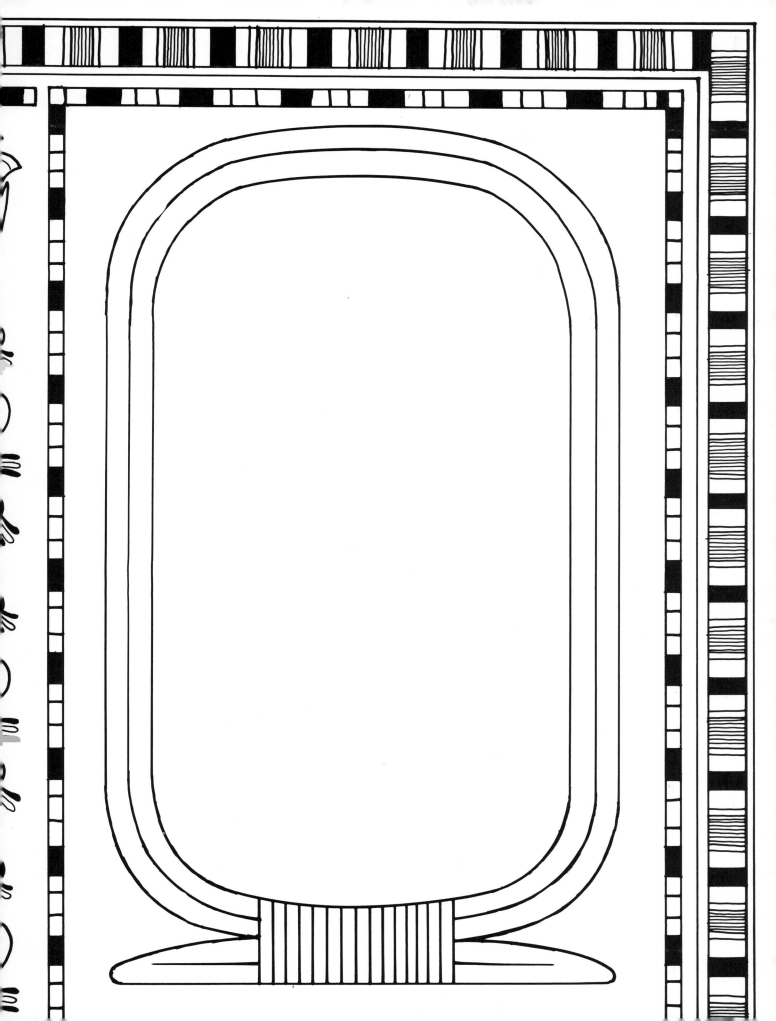

While on stakeout, Detective Jason spotted something very interesting.

© Susan Striker

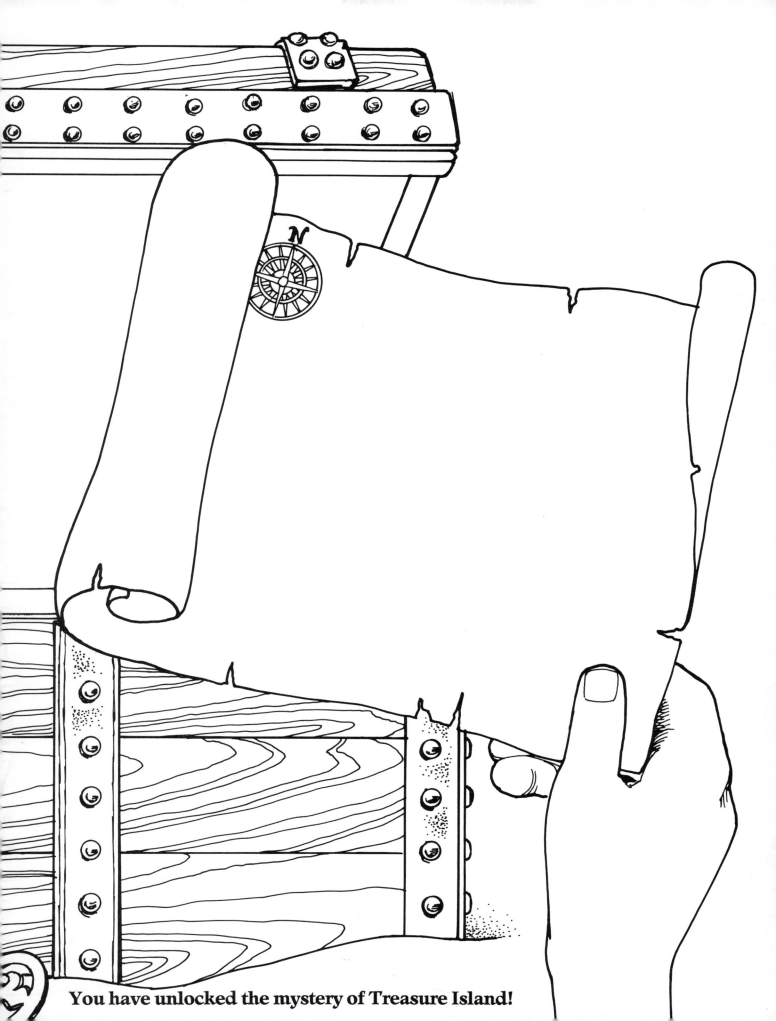

You have unlocked the mystery of Treasure Island!

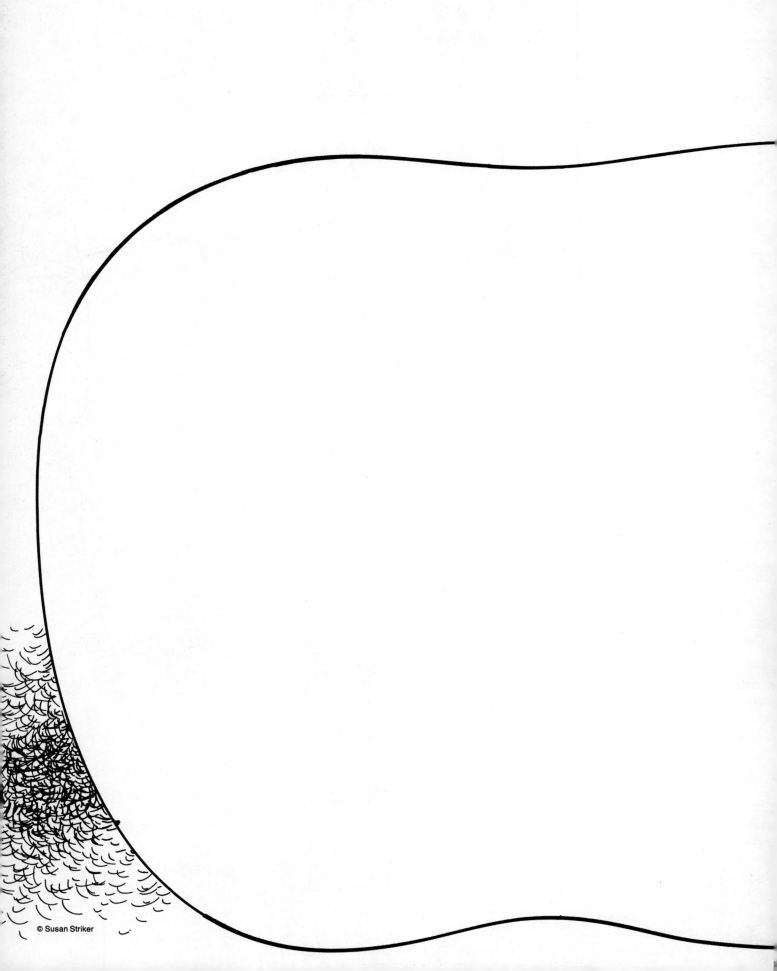

© Susan Striker

Only you can see the loot through the burglar's bag.

STOLEN VEHICLE REPORT

Check the appropriate box:

☐ Car   ☐ Truck   ☐ Boat   ☐ Trailer

INSTRUCTIONS: Print clearly and legibly
_____
Owner

_____
Address   Telephone

_____
Cost of vehicle

Physical description of vehicle:

_____

_____

_____

_____

Special features and equipment:

_____

_____

_____
Do you know who took the missing vehicle?

_____
Why?

_____
When?

_____

Draw a Picture of the Stolen Vehicle

You have been asked to fill out this stolen vehicle report.

© Susan Striker

Suddenly, the door

...opened to reveal...

What on earth can these frightened children be running from?

You have just made the first scientifically documented
sighting of the mysterious Loch Ness Monster.

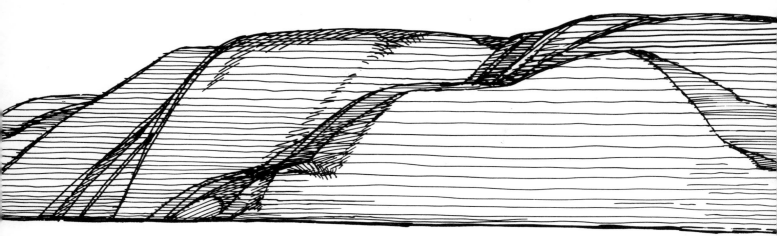

Uh oh! A spaceship has just landed in your backyard.
Draw it quickly before it disappears, so everyone will know what you see.

THE ANTI COLORING BOOKS®

A complete list.

The Anti-Coloring Book® by Susan Striker with Edward Kimmel
General interest, for ages 6 and older.
ISBN 0-8050-0246-4

The Second Anti-Coloring Book® by Susan Striker with Edward Kimmel
General interest, for ages 6 and older.
ISBN 0-8050-0771-7

The Third Anti-Coloring Book® by Susan Striker with Edward Kimmel
General interest, for ages 6 and older.
ISBN 0-8050-1447-0

The Fourth Anti-Coloring Book® by Susan Striker
General interest, for ages 6 and older.
ISBN 0-03-057872-8

The Fifth Anti-Coloring Book® by Susan Striker
General interest, for ages 6 and older.
ISBN 0-03-062172-0

The Sixth Anti-Coloring Book® by Susan Striker
General interest, for ages 6 and older.
ISBN 0-8050-0873-X

The Anti-Coloring Book® *of Exploring Space on Earth* by Susan Striker
Architecture and interior design.
ISBN 0-8050-1446-2

The Anti-Coloring Book® *of Masterpieces* by Susan Striker
The world's great art, including color reproductions.
ISBN 0-03-057874-4

Build a Better Mousetrap: An Anti-Coloring Book® by Susan Striker
Inventions, devices, contraptions.
ISBN 0-03-057876-0

The Mystery Anti-Coloring Book® by Susan Striker
Mysteries, Discoveries, and Cops and Robbers
ISBN 0-8050-1600-7

Look for these at your local bookstore.